MEGA
MELTDOWN

BIG PICTURE PRESS

First published in the UK in 2018 by Big Picture Press,
an imprint of Kings Road Publishing, part of the Bonnier Publishing Group,
The Plaza, 535 King's Road, London, SW10 0SZ
www.templarco.co.uk/big-picture-press
www.bonnierpublishing.com

1 3 5 7 9 10 8 6 4 2
0818 002

ISBN 978-1-78370-831-4

This book was typeset in Graham and Quicksand
Illustrations were created digitally using shapes, colour and texture

Written by Jack Tite
Consulted by Steve Parker
Designed by Jack Tite & Kieran Hood
Edited by Carly Blake & Tasha Percy-Baxter

Printed in China

MEGA MELTDOWN

Written & illustrated by Jack Tite

BPP

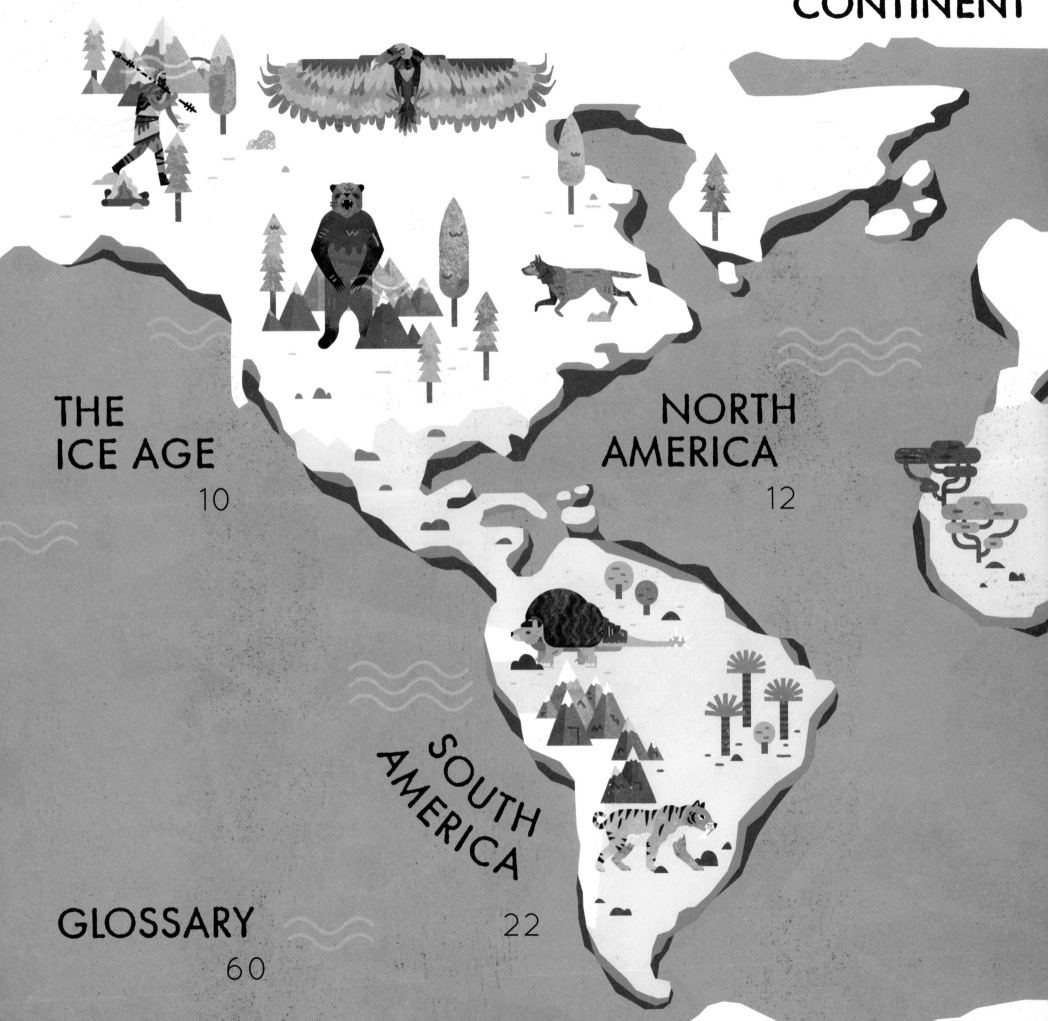

CONTENTS

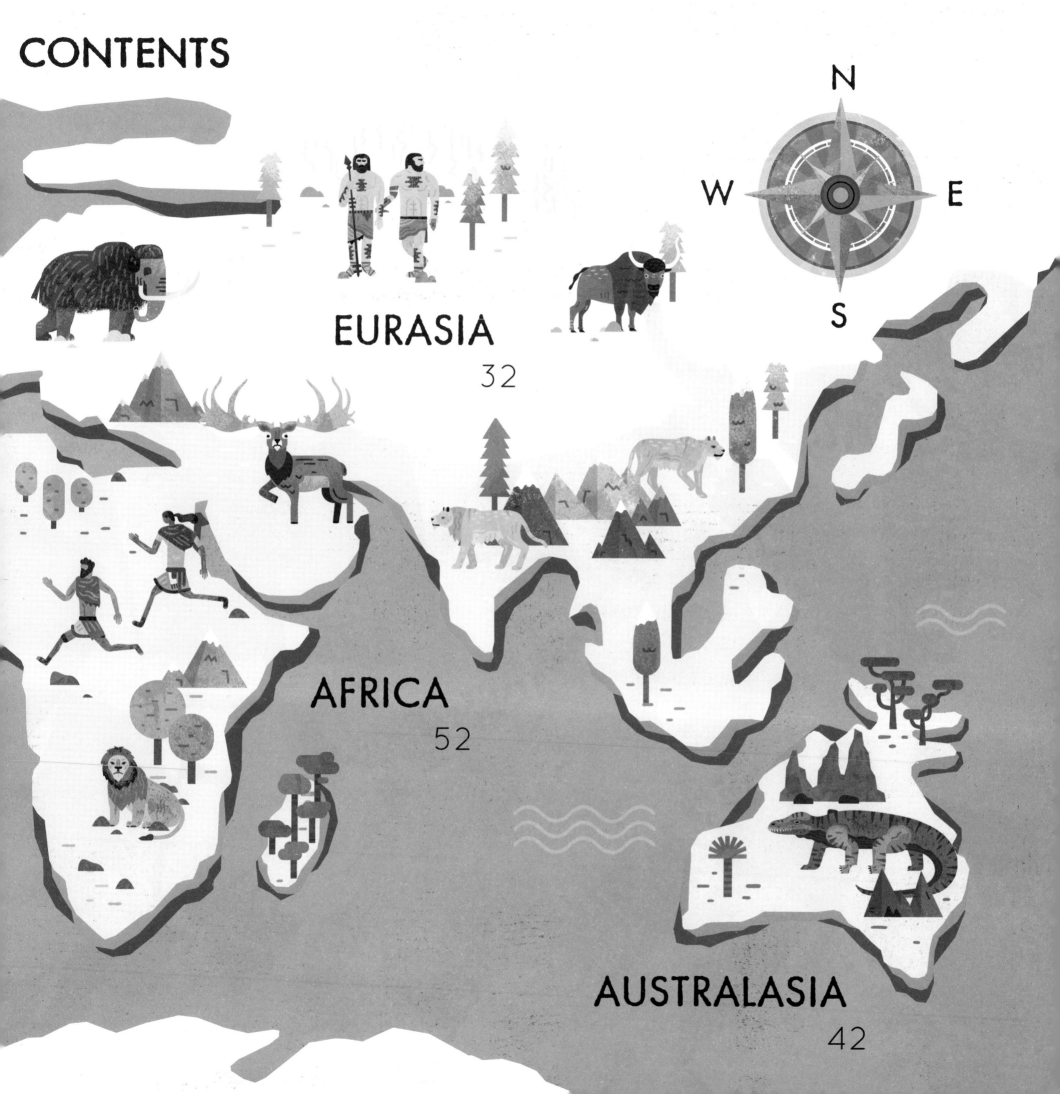

THE ICE AGE

Around 2.6 million years ago our planet began to change. Earth's temperature cooled, freezing the oceans and forming vast ice sheets over land, especially in the north. For the next 2.5 million years glaciers came and went in a series of ice ages. This long period of time is known as the Pleistocene epoch, or the 'Ice Age', and the creatures that roamed the land, swam in the oceans and soared in the air were truly enormous, weird and wonderful.

The Mega Meltdown

We know about these animals because of the mega meltdown that followed the Ice Age. Fossilised bones and even complete animals locked in ice, with their skin, fur and blood preserved, have allowed scientists to re-imagine the prehistoric animal world.

Early Humans

Our early human relatives appeared around the start of the Pleistocene epoch, and lived alongside the prehistoric animals in this book. Though conditions would have been harsh, early humans adapted, survived, evolved and spread. As the last glaciers began to melt about 15,000 years ago, people could venture into the previously deep-frozen lands of the far north.

Ice sheets covered continents and sea levels were lower

Most ice sheets have melted, so sea levels are higher

Changing Lands

With so much water frozen in glaciers and ice sheets, sea levels dropped, revealing bridges of land between continents such as North America and Asia. Both animals and humans travelled across these bridges, spreading into new territories. As the ice melted and sea levels rose, these routes were hidden again.

Supersized Animals

The supersized animals that lived in the Ice Age are known as Pleistocene megafauna (mega = large, fauna = animals). Beavers were bear-sized, giant sloths fought off sabre-tooth cats, huge birds filled the skies and hulking mammoths roamed the land. Get ready to journey around prehistoric Earth and come face to face with its inhabitants.

NORTH AMERICA

SHORT-FACED BEAR

The short-faced bear (scientific name *Arctodus*) is the largest bear ever to have existed. At 3.6 metres tall, it stood at double the height of an adult person and weighed as much as a small car. These bears were not only huge, they were also fast. Short-faced bears were capable of running as fast as a horse, reaching incredible speeds of up to 60 kilometres per hour.

Like many modern bears, these Ice Age giants were omnivores, meaning they ate both animals and plants, though meat made up the biggest part of their diet. Similarly to pandas, which feed on bamboo stems and leaves, short-faced bears had a bone in their wrists that enabled them to pick apart plants. *Arctodus* ate about 16 kilograms of food a day – enough to feed a person for a week.

Bone-Crushing Bite

The skull of *Arctodus* had a short snout in comparison to other bears. A shorter snout means more power, so we know this bear was capable of crushing bone with its jaws to get to the marrow inside. This tells scientists that *Arctodus* often scavenged for food.

Next of Kin

The short-faced bear became extinct 10,000 years ago. This may have been because other predators ate their food source, along with humans hunting them for fur and meat. The closest living relative and last of the *Arctodus* group is the spectacled bear, which lives in South America.

Bulky Bear

With long limbs, this bear was well equipped to run at speed to hunt. But its massive bulk would have been a burden when changing direction during a chase. The bear was too large to turn quickly, so agile prey could escape. When scavenging for food, it used its intimidating size to scare other predators away.

Monstrous Meals

Teratorns had large, hooked beaks and strong legs with sharp talons to hold down prey. A typical teratorn diet included live prey such as rodents, lizards and fish that could be swallowed whole. Even though these birds were able hunters, they would have scavenged for food where possible, using their gigantic size to scare off other animals. *Argentavis magnificens* could eat 10 kilograms of meat in a single day.

TERATORN

This monstrous family of birds existed from more than 31 million years ago to just 10,000 years ago. The biggest teratorn's wingspan measured a whopping 8 metres – twice that of the largest flying bird today. There were six species of teratorn, ranging in size, weight and physical features. Weighing as much as a wolf, *Argentavis magnificens* was the biggest. Scientists estimate it could dive at an astonishing 240 kilometres per hour, which is faster than most trains!

Baby Birds

Comparing teratorns to similar modern birds would suggest that *Argentavis* laid one or two eggs every two years, with hatching happening after 60 days of brooding. Chicks probably left the nest at around 16 months, but likely only reached their full size when they were 12 years old.

A large modern-day bird of prey would be dwarfed by a teratorn, as you can see from this scaled size comparison.

Argentavis magnificens

Bald Eagle

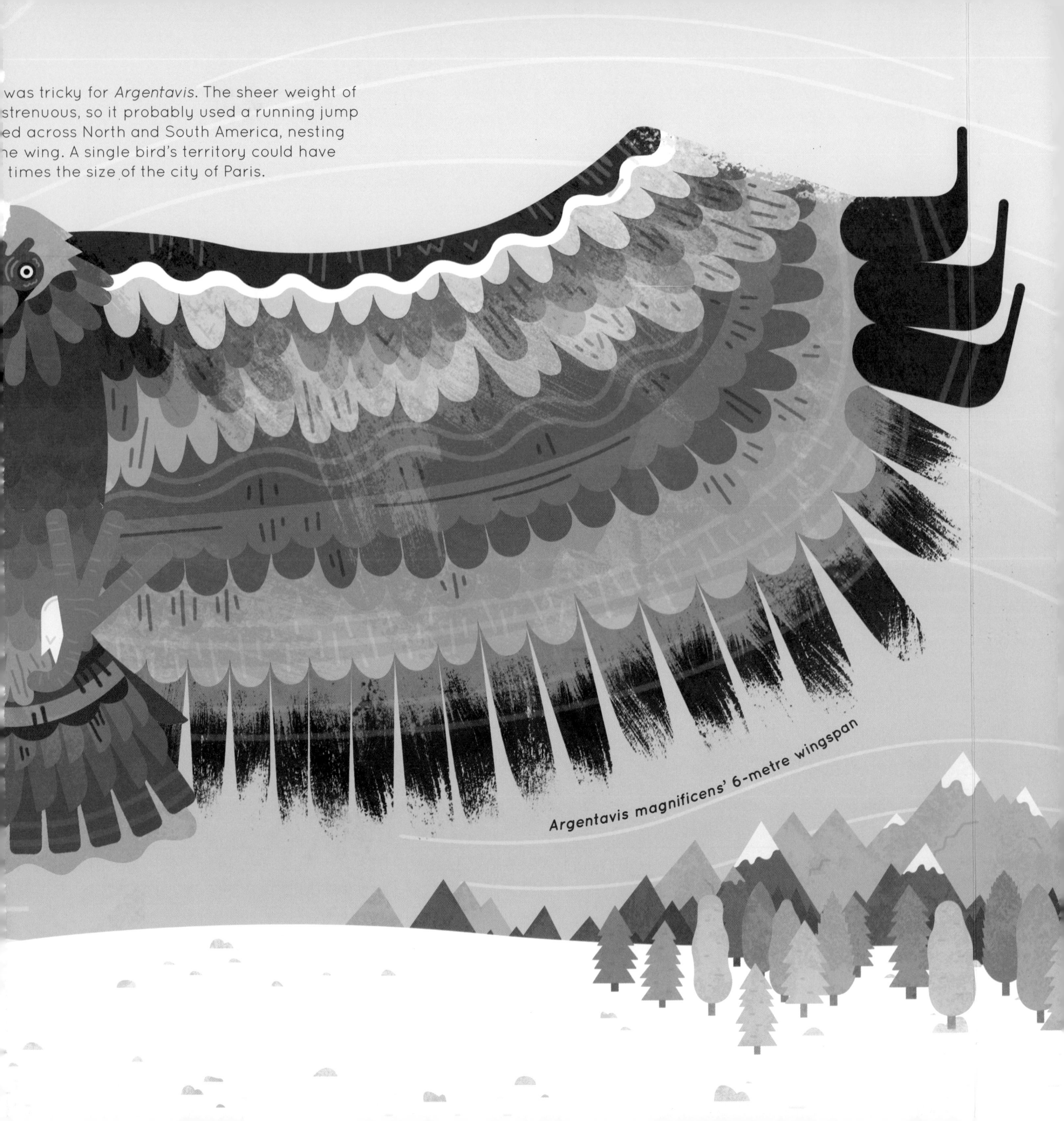

was tricky for *Argentavis*. The sheer weight of
strenuous, so it probably used a running jump
ed across North and South America, nesting
he wing. A single bird's territory could have
times the size of the city of Paris.

Argentavis magnificens' 6-metre wingspan

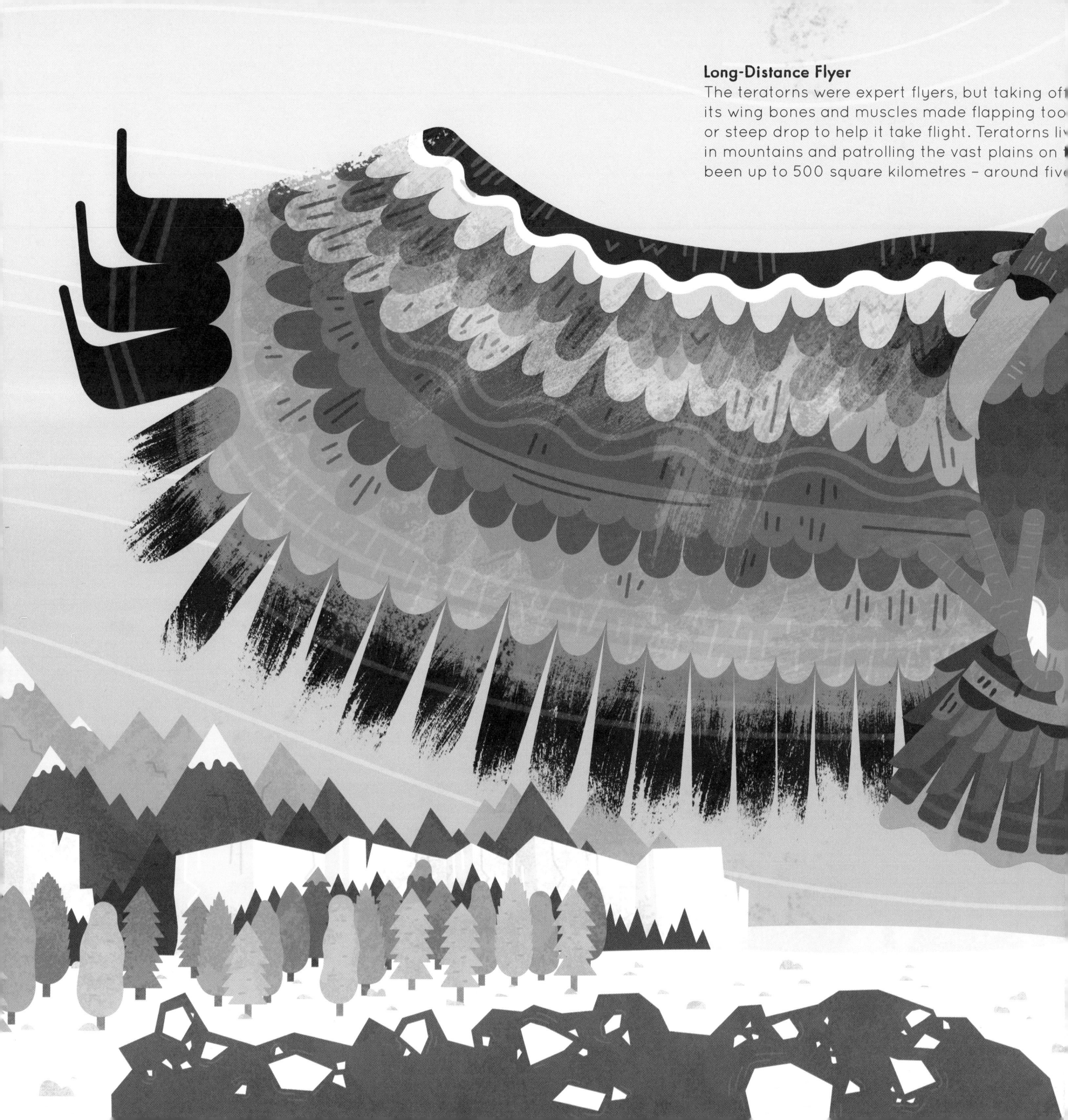

Long-Distance Flyer
The teratorns were expert flyers, but taking off
its wing bones and muscles made flapping too
or steep drop to help it take flight. Teratorns li
in mountains and patrolling the vast plains on t
been up to 500 square kilometres – around five

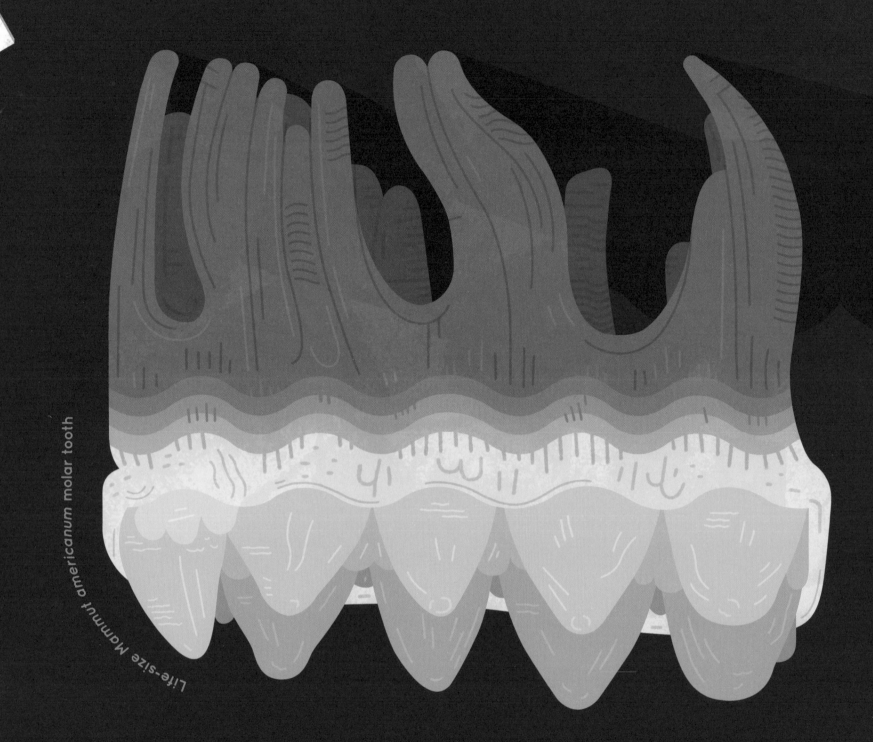

Life-size Mammut americanum molar tooth

Originally thought to have come from a race of 20-metre-tall giant humans, the molar was eventually shipped to London labelled 'Tooth of a Giant'. Nobody knew what prehistoric beast could have had such huge teeth, so they named the creature 'incognitum', or unknown species. In 1806 this was changed to mastodon.

In 1705, in the town of Claverack near New York, USA, a farmer dug up an unusual object. It was an enormous *Mammut americanum* tooth and it weighed the same as a small dog. This was the first ever mastodon finding.

MASTODON

Mega Mastodons

Mastodons are enormous prehistoric relatives of modern elephants and they first appeared some 20 million years ago. Scientifically known as *Mammut*, mastodons grew to 3.5 metres tall from foot to shoulder and weighed twice as much as an African elephant.

These mega creatures are usually upstaged by the better-known mammoth. Despite similar appearances, they were very different species.

Lone Rangers

Mastodons were forest-dwellers. Like modern-day elephants, scientists say females and calves lived in small families, whilst adult males were solitary. Males only gathered to fight, showing off their gigantic tusks, hopefully to impress a mate. Despite being nearly the size of buses, mastodons fed on branches and leaves, and used their tusks to reach up to the treetops.

Things Got Hairy

A mastodon's thick fur and bulky body kept it warm but also made it attractive to predators. Around 10,000 years ago mastodons became extinct due to a combination of overhunting, climate change and possibly a disease called tuberculosis.

GIANT BEAVER

Measuring 2.5 metres long and weighing as much as a panda, the giant beaver lived both on land and in water. Bones have been found in North America, and a legend from the Pocumtuc tribe of Native Americans tells of this rodent. A beastly beaver lived in a lake and emerged only to claim the lives of local people. They prayed for an end to the terror, until a spirit heard their plea and fought the beast. The spirit launched the beaver into the air, where it turned to stone. The beaver's head is said to have formed Sugarloaf Mountain in the Pocumtuc's local range in Maine, USA.

Terrific Teeth

Giant beavers (scientific name *Castoroides*) lived in lakes and woodlands in southeastern North America. They spent their days basking in water, eating aquatic plants and fending off predators with their 15-centimetre-long incisors. Their role in the ecosystem was more like that of a hippopotamus than a rodent.

Busy Beavers

Modern beavers are dam-building workaholics, well known for gnawing through tree trunks. They use twigs, stones and branches to build lodges and walls that block the flow of water. These structures contain food stashes and provide a protective, dry, well-hidden home.

Lodge

Baby beavers

Dam wall

Food stash

Here is a scaled size comparison of a *Castoroides* skull (right) and a modern beaver skull (left).

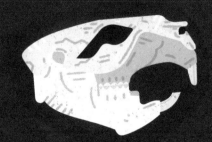
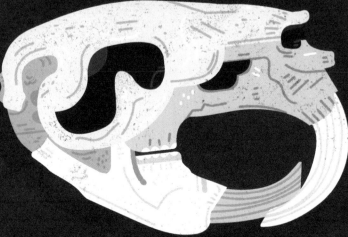

Where There's Water

Surprisingly, there is no evidence that giant beavers built dams. Their huge front teeth were too broad for chipping away at trees. Despite being 10 times bigger than its modern cousins, *Castoroides* was very adaptable, living in many parts of North America wherever there was water. Its kind thrived long enough to feature in legends, but went extinct with other North American megafauna at the end of the Pleistocene epoch.

SOUTH AMERICA

SMILODON

One of the best-known prehistoric animals is the sabre-toothed cat scientifically known as *Smilodon*. There were three species that lived across the Americas – *Smilodon gracilis*, *Smilodon fatalis* and the South American *Smilodon populator*, the last of which was the biggest. It was no larger than a lion, but it weighed twice as much at 400 kilograms, thanks to its stocky, bear-like build. Some scientists think these cats were social animals, living in family groups called prides, like lions today.

Smilodon's jaws could open to an angle of 120 degrees!

Armed to the Teeth

These carnivores earned their celebrity status because of their gigantic canine teeth, which grew up to 18 centimetres in length. These two teeth were so large that *Smilodon*'s jaws needed to open up to a huge 120 degrees to take a bite. In comparison, a lion's jaws only open to half that. Despite their bite, *Smilodon* was an ambush predator. It lived in woodlands and on plains, lurking under cover until prey was within striking distance. Using its strength and bulk, it would pin down prey and deliver a fatal bite or slash with its dagger-like canines. Surprisingly, *Smilodon*'s canines snapped easily and never grew back.

Smilodon prey in the Americas included:

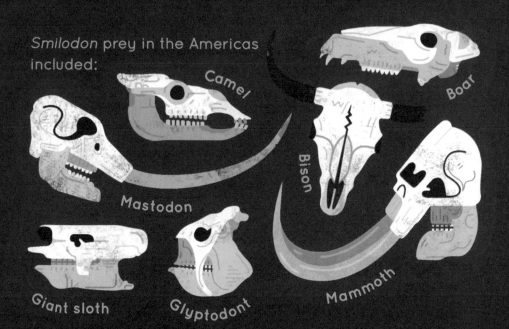

Camel

Boar

Bison

Mastodon

Giant sloth

Glyptodont

Mammoth

GIANT ARMADILLO

Car-sized *Glyptodon* was one of the biggest of the giant armadillos, or glyptodonts. The glyptodonts were close cousins of modern armadillos, but they were all gone by 10,000 years ago. Fossil evidence shows that they first evolved in South America and eventually ventured into North America, braving the freezing temperatures and scary predators. This diverse and once-common group contained more than 50 species, ranging from sheep-sized to as big as a Volkswagen Beetle.

Graze and Browse

Larger glyptodonts ate huge amounts of grass (this type of animal is called a grazer), whilst the smaller species ate roots and shrubs (this type of animal is called a browser).

Tough Armour

A glyptodont's shell is called a carapace. It was made up of 2,000 small, bony interlocking plates and each species had a different pattern. Glyptodonts couldn't tuck their heads into their shells, but they had bony head caps that could be used for headbutting.

A Good Shell-ter

Glyptodonts went extinct around 10,000 years ago. Early humans hunted them for their carapaces, which they used as shelters to protect them from the freezing weather.

Spots or Stripes?
Nobody knows what a *Smilodon*'s fur looked like. Scientists believe it was similar to that of lions', but it could have had spots, stripes or a different type of camouflage pattern.

A Change of Scenery
Smilodon dominated North and South America during much of the Ice Age, but by 10,000 years ago, all species were extinct. As the climate changed, woodlands gave way to open grasslands, which made stealthy hunting much more difficult. Not only did the gigantic prey *Smilodon* relied upon go extinct, but humans hunted these big cats, too, which sealed their fate.

Doedicurus' clubbed tail

Out Clubbing

Several kinds of glyptodont weighed over one tonne, but arguably the most fierce was 2-tonne *Doedicurus*. It had a long, clubbed tail with deadly spikes. A well-timed swing was powerful enough to break another glyptodont's carapace, and some males suffered this injury when fighting for females. *Doedicurus*'s tail also came in handy when defending itself against attacking predators.

Ruthless Rivalry

Giving its name to the glyptodont group, meaning 'carved tooth', *Glyptodon* itself lived near water and fed partly on aquatic plants – so battles for females could have ended with a splash! These giants didn't have club-like tails. Instead, they probably fought by crashing into each other. If a wounded *Glyptodon* rival was forced into the water, it would have been too weak to swim with the weight of its hefty shell and would have sunk to the depths.

Life-size pink fairy armadillo

From Mighty to Mini

The pink fairy armadillo is the smallest armadillo species. Believe it or not, this little desert dweller is among the closest living relatives of the long-gone glyptodonts!

LONG LLAMA

These strange-looking creatures belonged to a now extinct group of animals called litopterns. Long llamas were around 3 metres long and weighed one tonne – as heavy as a bison! They had a bizarre mixture of features – a nose trunk, the body of a humpless camel, long, thick legs and rhinoceros-like feet. Among the biggest litopterns were those in the group *Macrauchenia*, which translates to 'long llama'.

The Fast Lane

The Ice Age was a dangerous time for South American herbivores, but *Macrauchenia* was alert, agile and fast. These herd-living animals were capable of running at high speeds and changing direction quickly to outsmart predators. But if that failed, a long llama had one last option – a mighty kick with its powerful hind legs.

Nobody Nose

Macrauchenia's skull features nostril openings on top of the head. This confused eighteeth-century scientists, who thought that long llamas lived underwater and used their top-facing nose like a snorkel to breathe air. Scientists now think that *Macrauchenia* possessed a short trunk, which stopped dust getting up its nose and helped to grasp leaves, although this is widely debated.

A Joint Effort

Around three million years ago, the landmasses of North and South America had joined, and some animals spread from one continent to the other. This event is known as the Great American Interchange. Vicious predators from the north, such as stealthy *Smilodon* and tireless wolves, thrived on South American herbivores. Unfortunately, scientists think this, along with climate change and hunting by humans, led to the extinction of long llamas around 10,000 years ago.

Long llamas were mixed feeders, browsing in forests and grazing on grasses.

GROUND SLOTH

There were many types of ground sloth during the Ice Age. They evolved in South America and then spread to North America. Some were skilful burrowers, others had armoured scales and a few were even semi-aquatic. *Megatherium* was the group known as giant ground sloths, which were closely related to today's species. The largest, *Megatherium americanum*, grew to 6 metres long and weighed up to 6 tonnes – twice the size and six times as heavy as a polar bear.

Eat Your Greens

Giant ground sloths fed on any plants available, using their bulky tails and powerful back legs to balance upright like a tripod. With their towering height and long tongue, they were able to reach food from the tallest trees.

Dig In

Armed with 30-centimetre-long claws, giant ground sloths used their formidable fingernails to strip leaves from trees, dig up roots and defend themselves against predators. *Megatherium* isn't known for digging burrows and tunnels, but its relatives certainly did, as scientists have discovered ...

Going Deeper Underground

Remains of animal tunnels have been found in South America that are up to 20 metres long – that's as long as a seven-storey building is tall. The claw marks inside the tunnels are probably from Darwin's ground sloth, *Mylodon*, an Ice Age relative of *Megatherium*. The huge burrows protected ground sloths from the freezing temperatures and predators, and other creatures such as glyptodonts sheltered in them, too. Underground hide-outs were key to surviving the harsh weather conditions when animals migrated to North America.

A Balanced Diet

Some scientists say that giant ground sloths ate meat if there were no plants around. These giants may have hunted using their deadly claws or scavenged by scaring off animals from their kills.

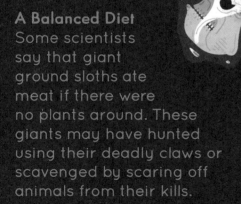

Sloth Survival

Around 10,000 years ago almost 90 per cent of sloth species went extinct, including the giants that roamed South and North America. Small ground sloths managed to survive in scattered populations on Caribbean islands until 4,200 years ago. Now, the tree-dwelling species such as the three-toed sloth are the last sloths left. These slowcoaches are much smaller than their ancestors, as you can see from this scaled size comparison.

Three-toed sloth

Megatherium americanum

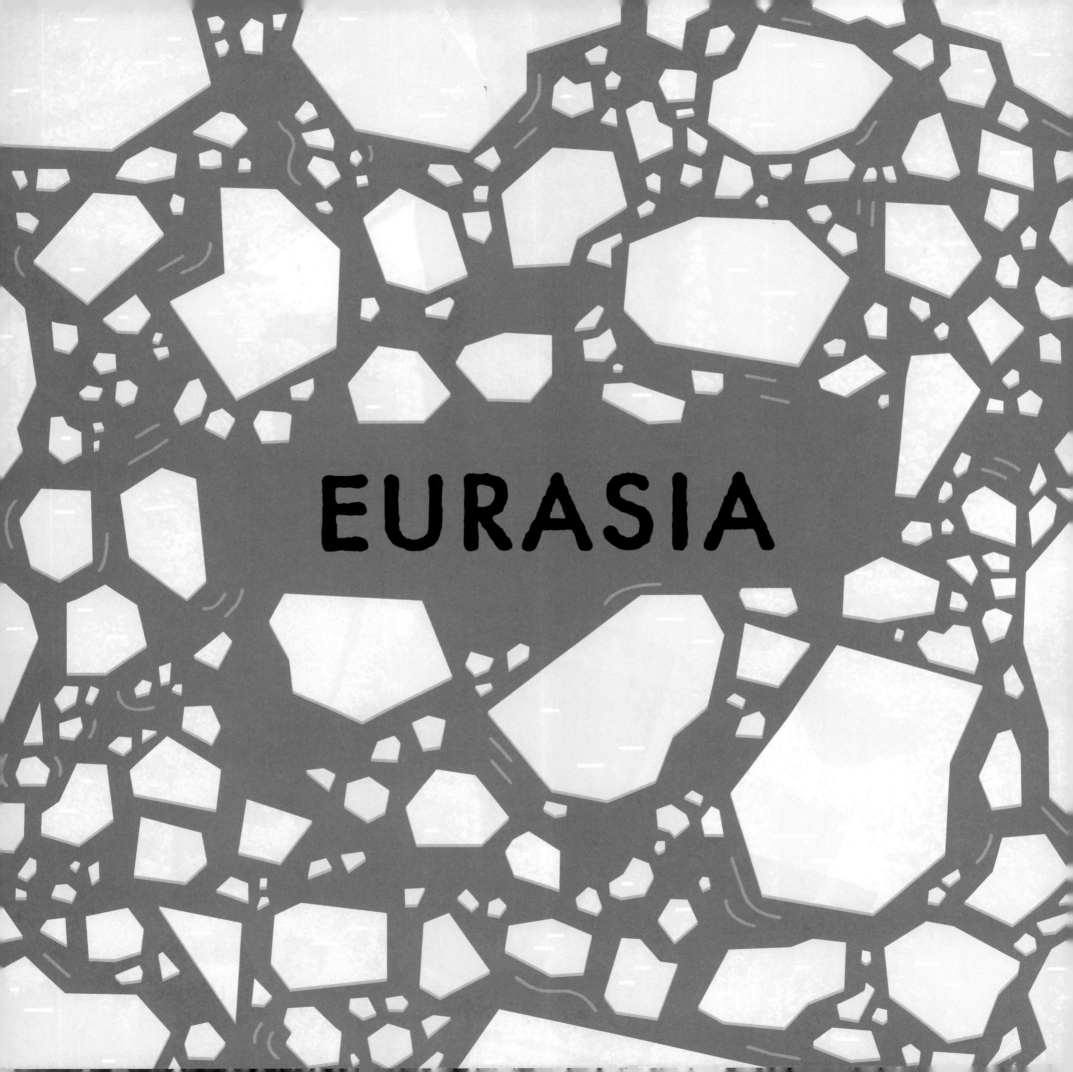

GIANT ELK

There are at least seven different species of huge Ice Age herbivores known as giant deer or giant elk, scientific name *Megaloceros*. The largest and most magnificent was *Megaloceros giganteus*. It stood 2.1 metres tall at the shoulder, and crowning the male's head was a pair of gigantic antlers with a span equal to the height of two adult people! A giant elk's antlers alone weighed 45 kilograms, which were supported by its strong neck. Like deer today, male giant elk shed their antlers each spring to regrow them for autumn, when they would clash in brutal battles to win over females.

Deer Distribution

Contrary to its name, *Megaloceros* was not an elk. It was a close relation of today's red deer, but with a thickset, moose-like body. Many well-preserved fossils have been found in bogs in Ireland, but we know giant elk lived all over Europe and parts of Asia. Irish mythology from the twelfth century mentions this huge deer, calling it *Fiadh Mór*, or the 'great deer', with antlers taller than a man.

Megaloceros stag and fawn

Long-Distance Deer

The giant elk had two things in its favour to escape predators – speed and stamina. Scientists say these moose-like animals could run great distances, wearing out predators brave enough to chase them. As they were social herbivores, travelling and grazing in herds like modern-day deer, giant elk probably chased off prowling hunters in groups to protect their vulnerable fawns.

Ancient Evidence

Ancient cave paintings of giant elk have been discovered all across Europe, which tell us how important these animals were to people as a source of food. Our Ice Age human cousins would have hunted tactically to take down these dangerous deer, driving them into dense forests where their antlers were too wide to fit between the trees, which made them easier to catch. Nobody really knows what led to the giant elk's extinction, but it survived in Siberia until less than 9,000 years ago.

Telling Tusks

Similar to trees, mammoth tusks have growth rings. Darker rings grew in winter and lighter rings in summer. From this, scientists can tell the age, health and even what season it was when the mammoth died. The largest *Mammuthus* tusk ever found belonged to a Colombian mammoth and measured a huge 4.8 metres long – the length of a great white shark! Items made from mammoth tusks have also been unearthed. A 42,000-year-old mammoth ivory flute is one of the oldest musical instruments ever discovered.

Mammoth ivory flute

A Giant Steppe for Mammoths

This is mammoth steppe – a vast feeding ground that spanned from Ireland in Western Europe, all the way east to where New York is today, in eastern North America. Many other animals roamed the steppe, such as woolly rhinos, bison and big cats.

New York

Gone But Not Forgotten

Many factors led to the woolly mammoth's demise around 10,000 years ago, including climate change and hunting by humans. However, small populations of dwarf mammoths managed to live on remote islands off the far northeast of Asia until as recently as 4,000 years ago (surviving until after the pyramids were built in Egypt). Although these animals are extinct, scientists think it may be possible to bring them back from the dead by using DNA from the well-preserved remains.

Woolly rhino

Woolly Wildlife

Mammoths weren't the only hairy megafauna. Shaggy-coated woolly rhinos were 3 metres long and armed with two huge horns for defense and attack.

Ireland

MAMMOTH STEPPE

Mastodon

Dwarf mammoth

Steppe mammoth

Woolly mammoth

WOOLLY MAMMOTH

The best-known celebrities of the Ice Age were the shaggy haired elephants of the genus *Mammuthus*. With a shoulder height of 3.6 metres and a weight of 6 tonnes, the woolly mammoth (*Mammuthus primigenius*) was hardly 'mammoth' compared some of its relatives. Steppe mammoths could reach 4.5 metres tall with a colossal weight of 12 tonnes, twice that of a *T. rex*! At the other end of the scale, there was a sheep-sized dwarf species. Woolly mammoths were perhaps the most supremely equipped for life in the freezing Ice Age.

Arctic Adaptations

Woolly mammoths had long, thick outer fur and a dense, short undercoat for warmth. Their shoulder hump stored extra fat for winter and their small ears helped reduce heat loss. It's also thought mammoths had 'antifreeze' blood, to withstand the sub-zero temperatures.

Fur layers

Mammoth molar

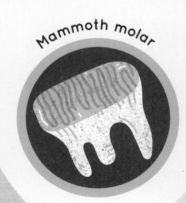

Something to Chew On

Mammoths' teeth were the most evolved of any elephant. Their large, flat molars had ridges to grind down tough plants. They went through six sets in their lifetime, regrowing a bigger and better pair when the old teeth became too worn. Mammoths probably used their huge curved tusks to clear snow and reveal the tasty green plants beneath.

Leg and foot bones

A Mammoth Appetite

With sturdy, pillar-like legs to support their hefty bodies, woolly mammoths travelled in herds searching for food, much like modern elephants. They were mainly grazers, eating up to 200 kilograms of food a day – that's heavier than an adult lion!

NEANDERTHAL

Homo neanderthalensis was the closest relative of our own species, modern humans, *Homo sapiens*. Neanderthals began to evolve more than 400,000 years ago across Eurasia. They lived in small, scattered groups, often in caves, where many of their fossilised bones have been found. Early discoveries of basic tools and study suggesting they spoke a primitive language led to the idea that Neanderthals were simple, club-wielding barbarians. However, we now know they were a highly intelligent and skilled people.

Cosy Homes

Neanderthals were adept at building and crafting. They used stone tools, animal bones and animal skins to construct sturdy shelters, with firepits inside, called hearths. Here are some of the many things Neanderthals made:

Crafting tools

Fire

Dugout canoes

Weapons

Natural remedies

Shelters

Jewellery

Plain Sailing

Some scientists say that Neanderthals sailed around the Mediterranean 100,000 years ago in simple boats or rafts – 50,000 years before humans took to the sea.

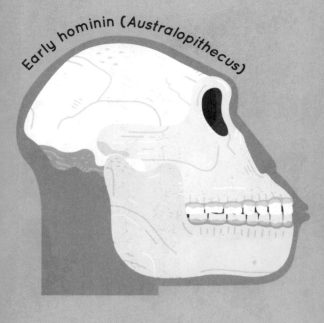

Early hominin (Australopithecus)

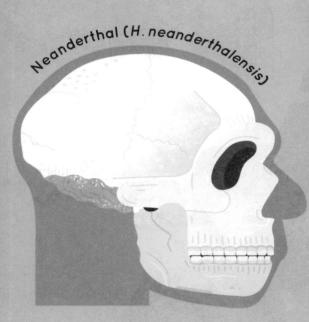

Neanderthal (H. neanderthalensis)

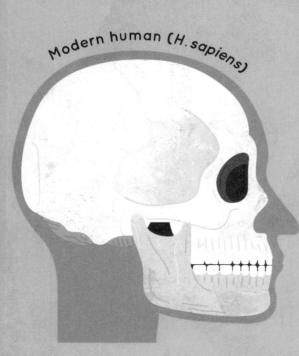

Modern human (H. sapiens)

Brain vs Brawn

Neanderthals belonged to a group called hominins, which include ourselves – *Homo sapiens* – and our earlier, more ape-like relatives. The well-developed skull of *Homo neanderthalensis* had large eye sockets, a heavy brow ridge and room for an astonishingly big brain. Surprisingly, a Neanderthal person's brain was bigger, on average, than that of a modern human. But some studies show that more of the Neanderthal brain was dedicated to body control and eyesight. This would have been favourable for Neanderthals' survival in the harsh conditions through the most extreme cold of the Ice Age.

Neanderthals Gone?

About 40,000 years ago, Neanderthals disappeared. Why? In Eurasia from around 50,000 years ago they encountered modern humans. Perhaps modern humans won the competition for food and other resources, or even attacked Neanderthals, but in other cases they joined together and had families. We know this because modern humans have, on average, about one to three per cent Neanderthal genetic material, DNA. In addition, the climate was warming and Neanderthals were best adapted to the deep freeze of the Ice Age.

The Big Hunt

From cave paintings to fossilised bones, there is plenty of
evidence that Neanderthals hunted many of the colossal
animals of the Ice Age, such as mammoths, woolly rhinos and
giant elk. To take down such large, powerful prey, Neanderthals
would have worked together in numbers, using rocks and
weapons such as spears in organised attacks.

A Mammoth Discovery

In 2012, a young boy named Yevgeny
Salinder was out walking his dogs in
North Russia when he stumbled upon
an extraordinary find . . .

. . . Yevgeny discovered a 48,000-year-old woolly mammoth skeleton, with skin, flesh and even a few organs still intact. The bitter temperatures meant the male mammoth had literally been frozen in time.

Neanderthal Anatomy

'Neanderthal' comes from the Neander Valley, in Germany, where quarry workers discovered a 'bear-like' skeleton in 1856. Scientists eventually declared the creature an ancient human relative, and since then many more bones and tools have been unearthed at the site. From this and many more finds, we know that Neanderthals stood shorter than humans, but were much stockier in build. They had a wide ribcage, flared pelvis, short legs and broad shoulders.

Living Off the Land

Similar to our modern diet, Neanderthal diet was dictated by where they lived and the food that was available at the time. On the Ice Age mammoth steppes, they hunted plenty of meat. In some parts of southwest Europe, they fed on forest moss, pine nuts and wild mushrooms. Some fossils show that Neanderthals also ate each other! However, this may have been part of a burial ceremony, rather than just being hungry.

Large brow ridge

Thickset build

H. neanderthalensis

Flat forehead

Taller in stature

H. sapiens

Slender build

Flared pelvis

Narrower hips

Large kneecaps

Long, slim limbs

This comparison shows the physical differences of *H. neanderthalensis* and *H. sapiens*:

Robust feet and hands

Behemoth Bears

Ursus spelaeus was a species of cave bear that lived across much of Europe and west Asia during the Ice Age. The fearsome males stood up to 3 metres tall and weighed half a tonne, although females were much smaller, weighing half that. Cave bears mainly fed on plants, seeds, berries and honey, but they occasionally hunted small mammals and scavenged other cave bears that had died.

Seeking Shelter

After a day spent foraging for fruit and raiding insect nests, these solitary bears returned to caves for cover. When the brutal Ice Age winter approached, they would venture deeper into cave tunnels to take shelter and hibernate, like some modern-day bears. This deep sleep helped cave bears to conserve energy and survive while food was scarce, but even hidden away deep in a tunnel they were not completely safe. There was one menacing predator that skulked in deep, dark caves, hunting these sleeping giants . . .

Cave bear

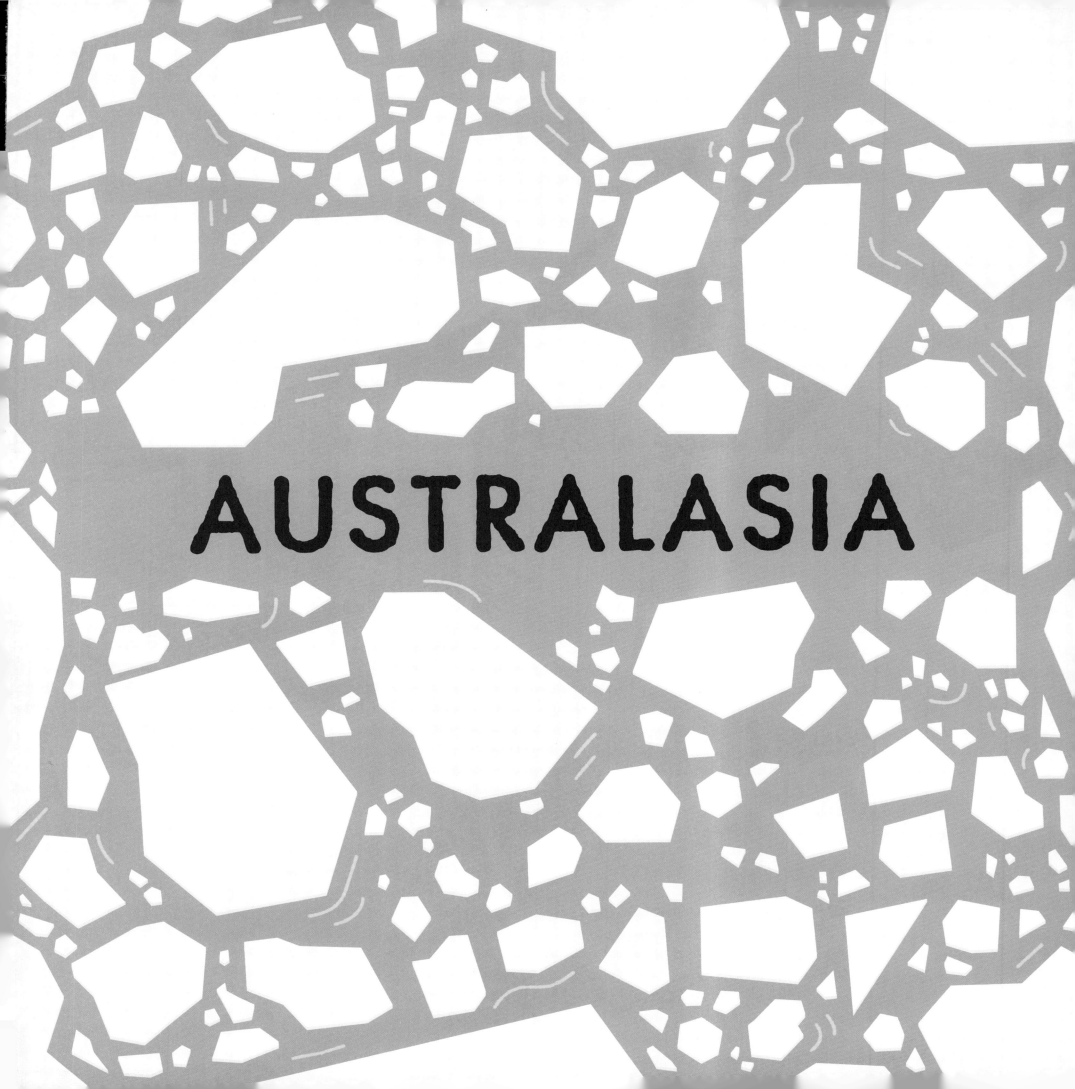

AUSTRALASIA

Cave lion skeleton

Carnivorous Cave Cats

Cave lions, scientifically known as *Panthera leo spelaea*, were 25 per cent bigger than lions today. Prehistoric cave art tells us that cave lions had neck manes and faint stripes, and that they hunted in prides, taking down horses, deer, bison and other large herbivores. In 2015, in northeastern Russia, scientists discovered a pair of preserved cave lion cubs who died at least 25,000 years ago, with inner organs, ears, fur and whiskers intact.

Sneaky Predators

The cave lion is so-called because many of its remains have been found in caves across Eurasia, but it actually lived in forests and grasslands. These predators preyed upon hibernating cave bear cubs, stealing them away whilst the adult slept. This might sound like an easy meal, but by the number of lion bones found in caves we can guess that it didn't always end well for these big cats!

Cave lion

Cackling Carnivores

Cave hyenas were bigger than today's African hyenas and they used their size to their advantage. They hunted large herbivores such as giant elks and woolly rhinos; even spear-wielding humans were sometimes on the menu! Travelling in groups and equipped with bone-crushing jaws, these spotty scavengers could scare Neanderthals and wolves away from their hard-earned food. Cave hyenas dragged their kills back into their cave dens to share the food with the group and eat in shelter.

Cave hyenas

A Picture Paints a Thousand Words

Ancient peoples left cave drawings in many parts of the world. These have helped scientists learn more about the relationship between humans and Ice Age animals. As the human population grew rapidly, people occupied more and more caves. This left other creatures without shelter, and, although this wasn't completely responsible for the animals' extinction, it probably helped seal their fate. Cave bears had become extinct by 20,000 years ago, cave lions had almost disappeared 15,000 years ago, and cave hyenas were gone by 10,000 years ago.

Other Cave Creatures

Scientists have explored caves all over the world, finding bones from Pleistocene animals such as ground sloths, wolves, leopards, mammoths, armadillos and even prehistoric turtles! On the Indonesian island of Sulawesi, cave art dating back some 40,000 years shows hand stencils and animal drawings.

H. sapiens

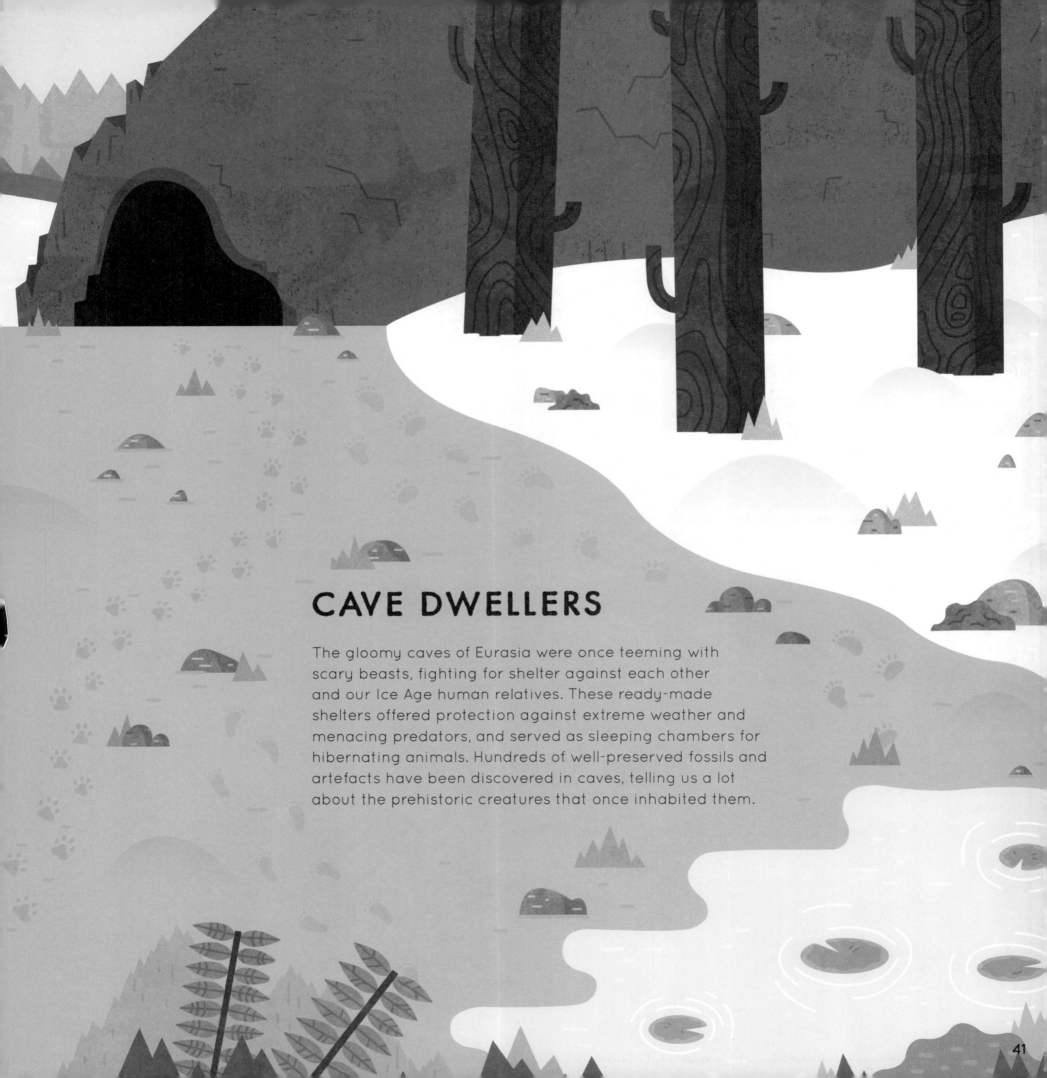

CAVE DWELLERS

The gloomy caves of Eurasia were once teeming with
scary beasts, fighting for shelter against each other
and our Ice Age human relatives. These ready-made
shelters offered protection against extreme weather and
menacing predators, and served as sleeping chambers for
hibernating animals. Hundreds of well-preserved fossils and
artefacts have been discovered in caves, telling us a lot
about the prehistoric creatures that once inhabited them.

Australia is home to a wide range of marsupial species: (left to right) koalas, tree kangaroos, numbats and bushtail possums.

GIANT WOMBAT

The giant wombat, or *Diprotodon*, was the biggest marsupial to ever live. It measured 3 metres from head to tail and weighed in at 3 tonnes – more than 30 times the weight of the biggest marsupial today, the red kangaroo! Marsupials are a group of pouched mammals found mainly in Australia. They are identified by a pocket-like flap of skin on their bellies, where the babies, called joeys, spend their first few months of life. Joeys are blind, deaf and hairless at birth, so these newborns instinctively climb to their mother's safe, cosy pouch. *Diprotodon*'s pouch faced backwards to stop dirt getting inside when the mother foraged or dug in the ground.

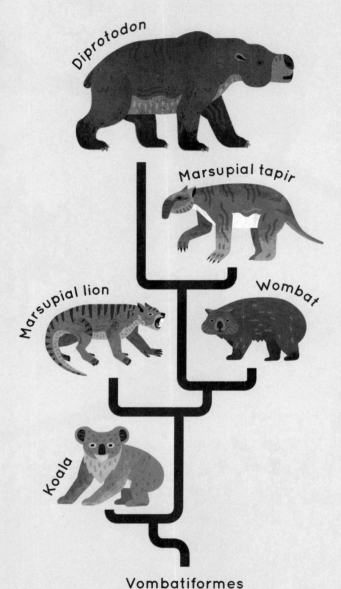

Diprotodon

Marsupial tapir

Marsupial lion

Wombat

Koala

Vombatiformes

Family Tree

There are more than 200 marsupial species in Australia today, such as kangaroos, koalas and possums. *Diprotodon* belonged to a group called Vombatiformes, which also included fearsome marsupial lions and horse-sized marsupial tapirs. According to the group's evolutionary tree, wombats and koalas are the closest-living relatives to these mighty marsupials.

On the Menu

Some scientists believe that *Diprotodon* lived in herds, although this idea is debated. Smaller females and their young were hunted by Australian predators, such as marsupial lions. The sheer size of adult males made them tough, but not impossible, to take down. Giant reptiles were capable of preying on the largest *Diprotodon* individuals.

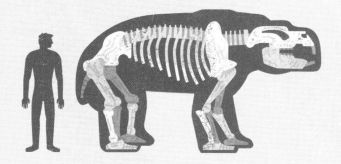

Roaming Far and Wide

Giant wombats lived all over Australia, roaming the plains in search of vegetation. It is estimated they ate up to 150 kilograms of shrubs and fruits in a day, about the same as an elephant eats! They used their large front teeth for plucking plants, like horses do, and their fist-sized molars for grinding food. As *Diprotodon* travelled in search of feeding grounds, it occasionally became trapped in soft lake mud, meeting a sticky end. At Lake Callabonna, in South Australia, hundreds of *Diprotodon* fossils have been discovered, well preserved by the muddy deposits.

Farming With Fire

The first people – ancestors of today's Aboriginals – probably arrived in Australia over 50,000 years ago. They discovered the unusual wildlife and hunted animals, including wombats, for an easy meal. They introduced fire-stick farming: setting fire to woodlands to clear a path and flush out animals to allow more of their own food plants to grow. Hunting and habitat destruction by humans, as well as tough droughts, slowly forced *Diprotodon* to extinction by 25,000 years ago.

MEGALANIA

There were many terrifying reptiles living in Australia during the last ice age, but one was more deadly than all the rest. Armed with huge claws, sharp teeth and armoured scales, giant ripper lizards, or *Megalania*, made the woodlands of Australia their hunting ground. By comparing *Megalania* to similar reptiles alive today, such as crocodiles, we know it would have able to take down animals 10 times its weight, but probably relied on ambushing prey because its top running speed would have been slow.

The Biggest Lizard

Megalania prisca wins the award for the largest land lizard ever. It measured up to a huge 7 metres long, or twice the length of a Komodo dragon!

One-Bite Wonder

Scientists believe that these lethal lizards had toxic saliva, like their living Komodo dragon relatives, meaning one bite would have been fatal. *Megalania* was also armed with a powerful tail, huge claws and serrated teeth to rip into its prey, such as large mammals and other reptiles.

Venom seeped from glands under the lower teeth

Giants

...ere plenty of reptiles that
...ongside giant ripper lizards
...he Ice Age. These included
...etre-long crocodile,
...a, giant snakes that lurked
...ring holes and strange-
...turtles with horns and
...tails, much like glyptodonts.

Rare Remains

Megalania prisca bones are
extremely rare finds. Vertebrae, single
teeth, lower jaws and limb bones have
been dug up, but scientists are yet to discover a
complete skeleton, meaning there is still a lot we don't know.
From dating the bones, scientists estimate giant ripper lizards
became extinct about 50,000 to 40,000 years ago, as the climate
changed and the animals they ate began to disappear.

Megalania baby hatching

Extraodinary Eggs

Komodo dragons are capable of something astonishing. With no contact from males, the females are able to lay eggs that hatch into young, and some scientists think giant ripper lizards could do the same. This means that small populations of Komodos can survive from just a few females, and this ability would have allowed *Megalania* to cling on to survival in small groups, even if numbers were low. However, there is one snag – the baby lizards born this way are almost all males.

Strange Sightings

Even in recent years there have been reported sightings of gigantic lizards lurking in Australia, appearing every now and then to devour farm animals. There is no solid evidence that giant ripper lizards are still alive, but some people believe that there may be a few living in the vast Australian outback or on remote Indonesian islands . . .

Terrific Taster

Megalania belonged to a group of large, fork-tongued lizards called monitors. These supersized reptiles would have tracked prey the same way modern monitors do. By flicking their tongue like a snake, they detected scents and tasted them using a special organ in their snout. A two-pronged tongue picks up a stronger scent on one side, which would have told the lizard which way to head.

Armoured Skin

On some body parts, giant ripper lizards had osteoderms – scales with embedded pieces of bone. So their skin was extremely tough, like chain mail worn by knights of old!

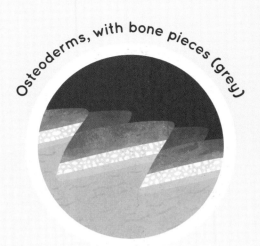

Osteoderms, with bone pieces (grey)

MARSUPIAL LION

These prehistoric predators were not actually lions – they belonged to a family of carnivorous marsupials called Thylacoleonidae and were more closely related to koalas than big cats. Some were squirrel-sized, but the biggest was the marsupial lion, *Thylacoleo*. It measured around 1.5 metres from head to tail and weighed up to 160 kilograms, heavier than a jaguar! With retractable claws, opposable thumbs and specialised teeth, marsupial lions were hyper-carnivores, preying on enormous Australian Ice Age mammals.

The Biggest Bite

Despite *Thylacoleo*'s modest size in comparison to other megafauna alive at the time, scientific studies have shown us that it had one of the strongest bites of any mammal, living or extinct. This meant it could have taken down prey much larger than itself, including giant wombats. A marsupial lion's teeth were highly specialised too, with huge incisors and unusually long back teeth, ideal for slicing meat. Some scientists think these carnivores were ambush hunters, stalking prey from hiding places such as overhanging branches, then striking with speed and killing their unfortunate victims.

The marsupial lion's teeth could stab and slice

A mother marsupial lion chases away her almost-grown offspring

Tough Love

These top carnivores were expert climbers but probably hunted mainly on the ground. Like most big cats today, they were most likely solitary animals. When a female marsupial lion had young she resided in a cave, sheltering her joeys from predators and teaching them how to climb on the rock faces. Like other marsupials, she had a pouch to carry and nurture her joeys. As the joeys became able to fend for themselves, it's possible the mother chased them away. This meant she could find another mate and have more young.

Without a Home

So, why would such an impressive predator go extinct? Unlike northern parts of the world, during the Ice Age Australia was minimally affected by the massive spreading glaciers and then the major meltdown. However, it was affected by climate change as conditions became warmer, more varied, and generally drier. Also, the newly arrived humans could have preyed upon the animals that marsupial lions ate. The introduction of fire-stick farming would have been another factor. Unable to feed or find a home, these fierce predators were on the way to extinction by about 40,000 years ago.

MOA

According to Māori legend, enormous flightless birds once roamed the forests of New Zealand. These birds were the moa. There were 10 or more species, and their preserved feathers show they varied in colour. The females of the biggest species stood at 3.6 metres tall and weighed the same as two ostriches! Moa had long necks and, like ostriches, would have held their heads close to the ground to search for low-growing greens. These big birds kept a lookout too, craning their neck to scan for their only predator (before humans arrived) – Haast's eagles.

Bush moa

South Island moa

North Island moa

Haast's eagle

Coastal moa

Upland moa

Eastern moa

Moa eggs

Upland moa foot

Egg-Cellent Parents
Female moa were much bigger than the males and more than twice as heavy. Scientists think that after a female laid her eggs, the male took care of them while she went to forage. This is because eggshell fossils show the shells were too thin to have taken the female's weight. While foraging, moa ate twigs, berries, leaves and occasionally sharp rocks and gemstones. These stones are called gastroliths, and they stay in a part of the gut called a gizzard and help to crush food into a pulp. This is common in birds, because they don't have teeth to grind up food.

A Special Find
In 1986, scientists were exploring the gloomy caves of New Zealand's South Island when they stumbled on a remarkable find – a 3,000-year-old upland moa foot with scales, claws and flesh still preserved!

No Meal Too Big

Haast's eagle, or *Harpagornis moorei*, was the largest eagle ever to have lived. It weighed up to 15 kilograms, nearly twice as much as the heaviest eagles alive today, such as Steller's sea eagle. Haast's eagles were the top predators of New Zealand at the time, with bone-puncturing talons the size of tigers' claws, short wings for navigating through the dense forests and a broad beak. This daring carnivorous raptor hunted the mighty moa, despite it being ten times the eagle's own size.

A Haast's eagle swooping on a moa

Deadly Diver

It's thought these terrifying birds of prey could have swooped down at up to 80 kilometres per hour, striking moa to the ground. Scientists have found lots of moa skeletons with holes that are an exact match to the talons of Haast's eagles.

Two Birds with One Stone

Humans first arrived in New Zealand in the thirteenth century. They hunted moa for food, destroyed their habitat and introduced animals that preyed on moa eggs. By the end of the same century, moa had all vanished, and with no prey to eat, Haast's eagles met the same fate soon after.

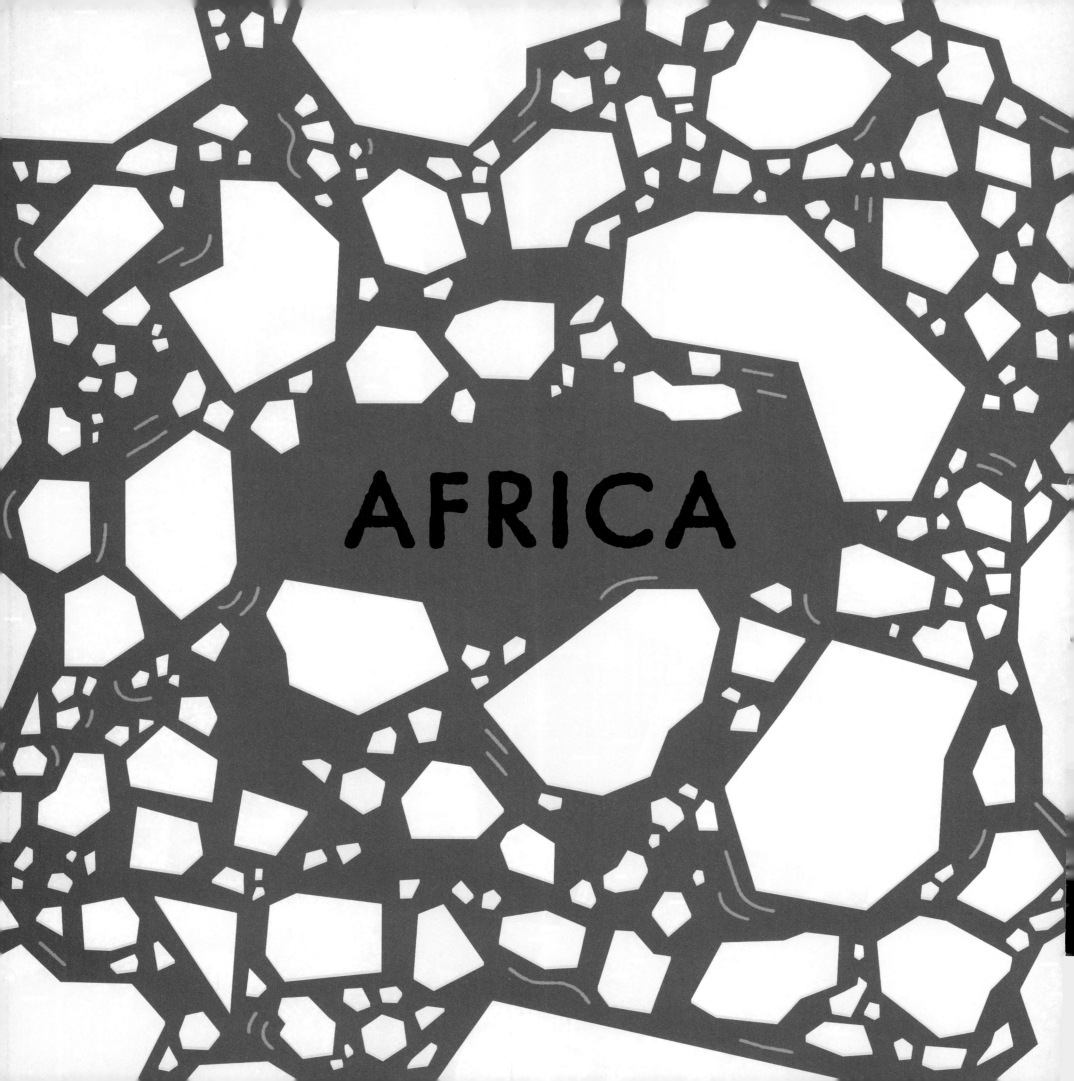

EARLY HUMANS

All people alive today belong to our species known as modern humans, or *Homo sapiens*. To talk about our origins, we have to go far back in time. Around a million years ago, earlier species, such as *Homo erectus* and then *Homo heidelbergensis,* populated Africa, Asia and Europe. From about half a million years ago, some of these earlier humans in Asia evolved into a group called Denisovans, and others in Europe became the hardy Neanderthals. It was in Africa that our own species began, which would go on to dominate and shape the world.

Ancient Relatives

In 2017, the oldest-known modern human fossils were discovered in North Africa. This discovery pushed back the origins of *H. sapiens* to 300,000 years ago – 100,000 years older than scientists previously thought, and deeper into the Pleistocene ice ages. This incredible find will help the study of our origins, but it also raises many new questions.

Human Habitat

During the Ice Age, Africa did not endure huge spreading glaciers and long winters. But it did go through several periods of climate warming and cooling, becoming very dry at times. Some scientists thought that as the changing climate transformed much of Africa into a dry desert, early modern humans survived in a small area, dense with vegetation and animal life. However, fossils now suggest that modern humans arose across many parts of Africa.

Brainy Benefits

The first modern humans evolved leaner limbs and a lighter skeleton than their predecessors. The human skull changed dramatically, too, developing a smaller brow ridge, a flat forehead and a larger brain. This brain is what makes us truly unique, and it allowed early modern people to thrive, make new tools and become the first human species to spread all over the world.

Cutting-Edge Technology

As modern people spread and continued to evolve, they crafted complex tools and weapons never seen before. They were also armed with increasing knowledge, helped by language. This allowed humans to communicate with each other and hunt in groups, which introduced a range of animals into their diet. People also developed more kinds of art – they created cave drawings using paints made with charcoal and ocher (red clay) and crafted decorative ornaments.

OUR JOURNEY

Luckily, our modern human relatives survived the Pleistocene ice ages. Several times in the past half a million years, and most recently by about 70,000 years ago, they migrated out of Africa. Along these journeys, they encountered Neanderthals, Denisovans and perhaps other hominins. They had families with some, but continuing as *H. sapiens* they went on to spread all over the globe.

In each region, as they came across enormous animals, they crafted more complex weapons and tools to hunt larger prey and kill off huge predators. These early explorers reached Australia by 50,000 years ago and later travelled all the way to South America over a land bridge between Asia and Alaska by roughly 15,000 years ago. This completed our worldwide expansion, but the journey didn't end there . . .

EURASIA

AFRICA

Modern Megafauna

Africa is the only continent on Earth where a diverse range of animals approaching Ice Age-sized megafauna can still be found. Elephants, hippos, rhinos and giraffes are just a few of the great survivors that still roam the savannah. They seem big to us, yet we know the Ice Age relatives of these animals were even more huge.

TO NORTH AMERICA

The Grass is Greener

The human population rocketed 10,000 years ago, as our ancestors learnt how to domesticate animals and grow their own crops. Humans also began to settle in fixed places, spending more time farming than hunting.

AUSTRALASIA

Today, human activity is affecting the environment and climate, making it difficult for many animals to live.

Explorers Everywhere

Over hundreds of thousands of years, from cave people to seafaring Vikings and pirates, human explorers have spread far and wide, inhabiting every continent, except Antarctica. Today, there are even humans living in space on the International Space Station, which orbits Earth. Our story continues with you and all the people alive today.

Fossils and Clones

New fossils are still being unearthed all over the world, giving us more insights into the past. Mummified moa and frozen mammoth remains, complete with preserved genetic material, may provide scientists the opportunity to bring these prehistoric wonders back to life one day, in processes such as cloning and 'de-extinction'.

In Danger Today

Most of the creatures of the Ice Age are well and truly extinct. Animals at risk of extinction today are called threatened species and some of the reasons they become threatened are the same as for prehistoric megafauna: climate change, which results in rising sea levels and warming oceans; deforestation, which destroys habitats and food sources; and hunting, which dwindles numbers further. Thousands of species are at threat today, including:

Komodo dragons

Pangolins

Red pandas

Hawksbill turtles

Elephants

Gorillas

Bluefin tuna

Orangutans

Tigers

Back from the Brink

Thanks to the tireless efforts of people who work in conservation, there have been success stories. In 2016, tiger numbers rcse for the first time in 100 years and the giant panda was listed as no longer endangered for the first time in 50 years. This proves that we can make a difference to preserve the incredible animals on this planet.

GLOSSARY

Adaptation – Changing, or adapting, in order to better suit the environment and other conditions.

Ambush – A surprise attack from a hidden position.

Ancient – Dating back to the distant past, usually up to the end of the Roman Empire.

Antler – The branching structure that usually grows on the heads of animals such as deer.

Aquatic – Living permanently or mostly in water.

Browse – To feed on various high-growing plants, including fruits, twigs, leaves and shrubs.

Burrow – A tunnel dug out by an animal and used for a home or hiding place.

Cache – A collection of items, such as food, hidden away for future use.

Canine – A long, pointed tooth between the incisors and premolars of a mammal, often enlarged in carnivores for eating meat.

Carapace – A protective tough outer covering of animals such as tortoises and crabs.

Carnivore – An animal that feeds on other animals. Tigers, lions and wolves are carnivores.

Climate – The average long-term weather conditions in a region or over a period of time.

Denisovan – An extinct human species originally found in Siberia that lived during the Ice Age.

Endangered – A species at risk of extinction, such as the polar bear.

Epoch – A specific period of time marked by some kind of big change or event.

Extinct – When a type of animal or plant has no more living members, such as woolly mammoths.

Feline – An animal belonging to the cat family or animal with cat-like characteristics.

Fossil – The remains of a living thing such as a plant or animal, usually preserved in rock.

Gastrolith – A stone swallowed by an animal to help grind food into a pulp in the gut.

Glacier – A huge body of ice that usually moves extremely slowly, like a very slow frozen river.

Graze – To feed on grass.

Great American Interchange – The movement of land animals and plants between North and South America, when they were joined by a land bridge 3 million years ago.

Herbivore – An animal that only eats plants. Elephants and giraffes are herbivores.

Hominin – A member of a group that includes all humans and their earlier relations, after they evolved separately from other great apes.

Homo heidelbergensis – A now-extinct kind of human, possibly the ancestor of our species.

Homo neanderthalensis – A hardy, now-extinct type of human that survived recent ice ages.

Homo sapiens – The only living human species, to which all people today belong.

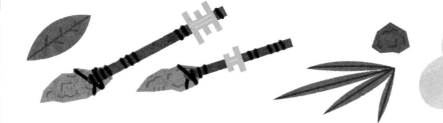

Hypercarnivore – An animal, usually a top predator, with a diet that is all, or almost all, meat.

Incisor – A narrow, flat-edged tooth adapted for cutting, and useful for eating plants.

Ivory – The substance that the tusks of animals, such as elephants or walruses, are made of.

Joey – A young kangaroo or other marsupial that still relies on its mother.

Litoptern – A group of extinct South American hoofed mammals with one or three toes.

Marsupial – A type of mammal that usually has a pouch to protect and feed its young in.

Megafauna – Very large animals with a body weight of 40 kilograms or more.

Migrate – When animals travel a great distance from one place to another according to seasons or to move to new lands.

Molar – A tooth at the back of an animal's mouth for grinding and crushing food.

Mummify – To preserve a body by drying it out. This happened naturally to some Ice Age animals when they died and became frozen in the ground.

Mythology – A set of stories that belong to a particular religion or culture.

Omnivore – An animal that feeds on both plants and other animals.

Organ – A part of the body that performs an important function, such as the heart.

Ornament – A decorative item that has no practical use other than to look attractive.

Osteoderm – A bony plate found in the skin of animals such as crocodiles.

Plains – Large, fairly flat areas of land, usually with grass or low plants but few or no trees.

Pleistocene – The time period ranging from 2.6 million to 11,700 years ago.

Predator – An animal that hunts and kills animals for food, e.g. lions or sharks.

Prey – An animal that is hunted, caught and killed by another for food, such as rabbits or deer.

Remote – A place that is hidden away or cut off from the rest of the world.

Reptile – A group of backboned, cold-blooded, mostly egg-laying animals with scaly skin, such as crocodiles.

Retractable – When something can be drawn back in. For example, a cat can retract its claws.

Scavenger – A creature that eats dead animals it has not killed itself.

Species – A group of closely related, similar living things that can all breed together.

Thrive – When an animal or plant grows well and is healthy and successful.

Toxic – Containing something poisonous or venomous and likely to cause death or injury.

Tuberculosis – A serious bacterial disease that can lead to death.

Vegetation – Trees, flowers, grasses and other plants in a specific area.

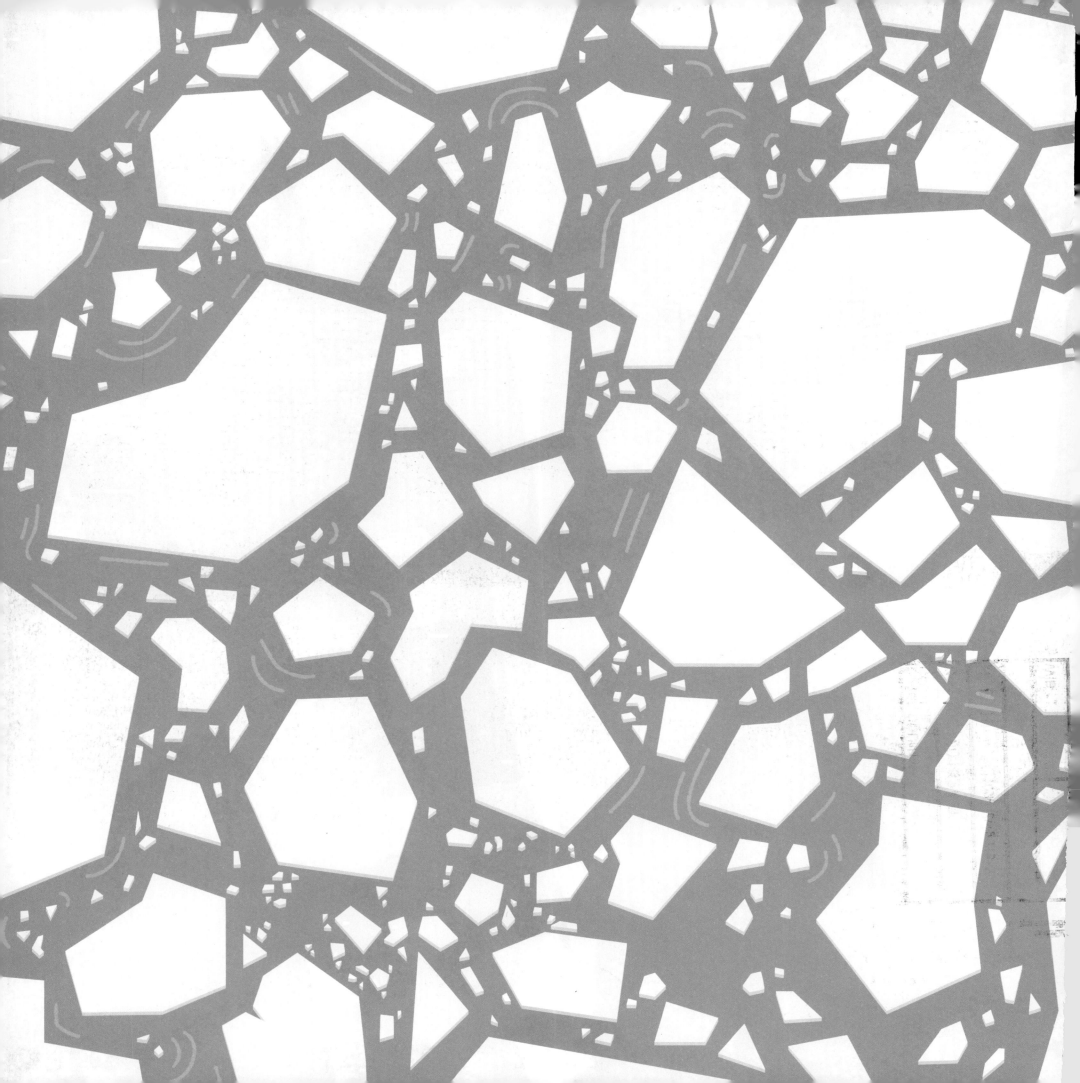